The United Empire Loyalists & You

By the President of the Nova Scotia Branch of the United Empire Loyalists' Association of Canada

BRIAN MCCONNELL

DEDICATION

*To the memory of the United Empire
Loyalists who settled in Nova Scotia*

CONTENTS:

1. WHY DO THE UNITED EMPIRE LOYALISTS MATTER?

By 1784 after the end of the American Revolution an estimated 40,000 refugees who had remained loyal to Britain and King George III had arrived in Canada. They are now known as United Empire Loyalists. Their arrival led to the creation of the separate provinces of New Brunswick, named after the House of Brunswick of which King George III was descended, and Ontario. These refugees came from many cultures and ethnic backgrounds including English, Irish, Scottish, German, Dutch, and African.

Map of Nova Scotia, New Brunswick & Cape Breton, published October 10, 1794 by J. Stockdale, Piccadilly, England. Author: Morse, Jedidiah.

In Halifax Harbour at Dartmouth, Nova the Eastern Battery had been built. It was a fortification to help protect the area. Over 500 soldiers who were members of the King's Orange Rangers were stationed there during American Revolution. This was a regiment formed in 1775 in Orange County, New York from Loyalist volunteers. A Company was also sent to Liverpool. At the end of the American Revolution the regiment was disbanded and many settled in Nova Scotia.

Ships preparing to depart for Louisbourg in 1757. Eastern Battery appears on right.

At the Old Burying Ground in Halifax there are graves of many Loyalists including John Howe (1754 - 1835) who had been a Printer in Boston prior to the American Revolution. He supported the British Crown and departed for Halifax. Howe arrived at Halifax in 1779 and set up a printing shop, where he published the first issue of the *Halifax Journal* in December 1780. In 1801, Howe was rewarded for his loyalty by appointment as the King's Printer and in 1803 he became deputy postmaster for Nova Scotia, New Brunswick, and Prince Edward Island.

Gravestone of Loyalist John Howe in Old Burying Ground at Halifax, NS

The son of John Howe was Joseph Howe (1804 - 1873), who became a prominent journalist, politician and public figure in Nova Scotia. He was also responsible for establishing the right of a free press in Canada. It has been observed that *"the most lasting influence upon Howe was exercised by his father, loyalist John Howe, whom he once described as "my only instructor, my play-fellow, almost my daily companion." The one member of his family who sided with Britain in revolutionary times, John Howe had a reverent, almost mystical, attitude towards the British connection, and he passed this attitude on to his son."* (1)

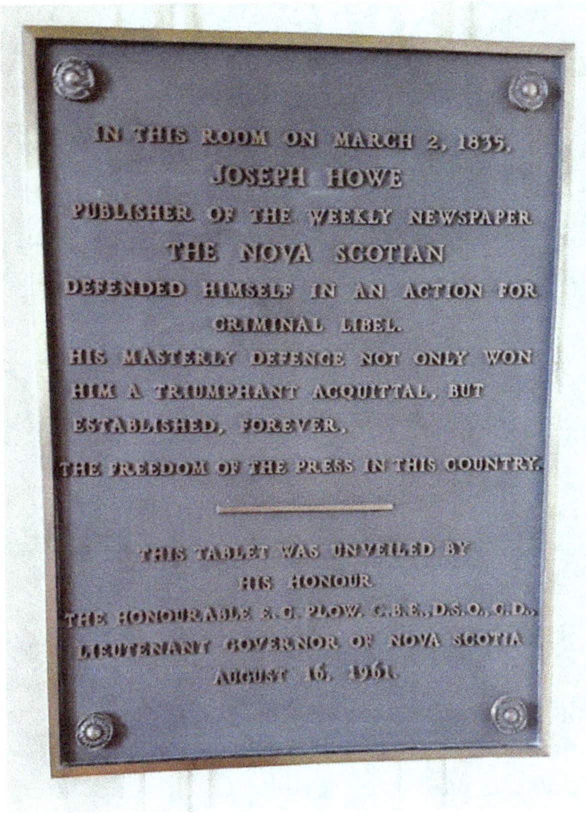

(1) Beck, J. Murray, "HOWE, JOSEPH," in Dictionary of Canadian Biography, vol. 10, University of Toronto/Université Laval, 2003–, accessed October 13, 2018, http://www.biographi.ca/en/bio/howe_joseph_10E.html

A Map prepared by members of the Nova Scotia Branch of the United Empire Loyalists' Association of Canada highlights the areas of Loyalist settlement in Nova Scotia. It also indicates museum locations with a Loyalist theme.

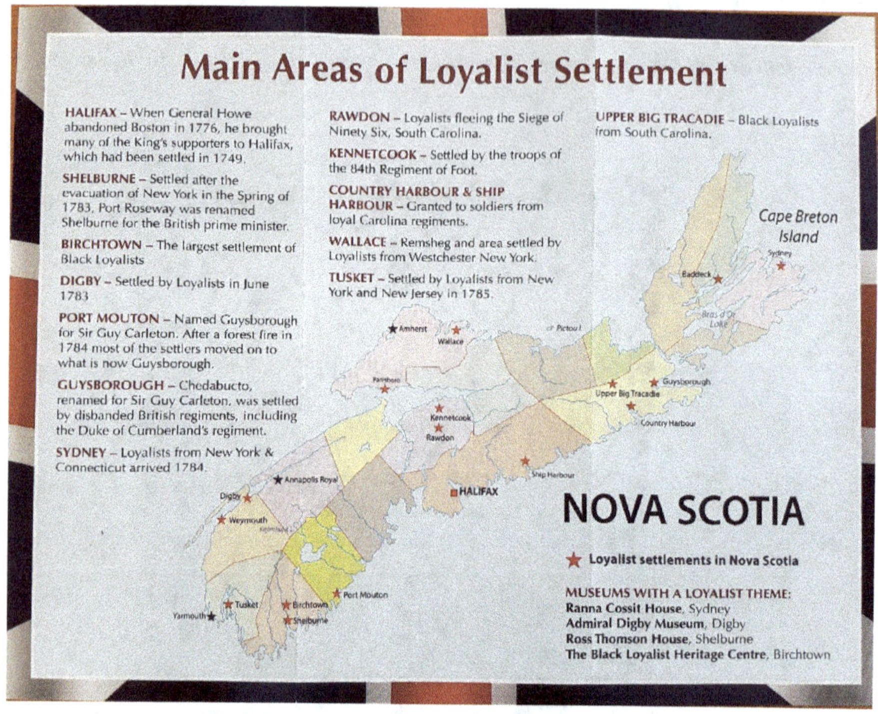

The Loyalists who arrived in Canada were refugees. Through the conflict which has become known as the American Revolution many had lost all or most of their personal possessions. Some called them British Tories. However, as well there were native people like the Mohawks who went north to Canada and different racial groups as with the approximately 3,000 Black Loyalists who came to Nova Scotia. (2)

(2)"The Black Loyalists: The Search for a Promised Land in Nova Scotia and Sierra Leone 1783 - 1870", by James W. St. G Walker, New York: Africana Publishing, 1976

The Loyalists were Canada's first Multi- Racial refugees.

Painting of a Black Loyalist in Shelburne, Nova Scotia (3)

New Brunswick was created in 1784 as a separate colony from Nova
Scotia when discontentment with the government in Halifax by Loyalist
refugees led to its creation north of the Bay of Fundy. Previously it had
been inhabited by indigenous people, the Maliseet, Mi'kmaq and
Passamaquoddy, for thousands of years until European explorers came.
The French and English competed for the area during the 1600s and
early 1700s until the Treaty of Utrecht in1713 awarded it to Britain. It
became part of the colony of Nova Scotia. Cape Breton was also
created as a separate colony in 1784 due to the Loyalists settling there,
however, in 1820 it rejoined Nova Scotia.

(3) "King's Bounty: A History of Shelburne, Nova Scotia", by Marion Robertson,
Nova Scotia Museum, 1978

The two Loyalist communities of Parr Town and Carleton established on either side of the mouth of the Saint John River were amalgamated into the first city to be founded in Canada. On May 18, 1785 the city of Saint John was proclaimed by Royal Charter granted by King George III.

An influx of Loyalists into the part of Lower Canada (present day Quebec) mainly along the St. Lawrence River to the Bay of Quinte and in the Niagara Peninsula led to the creation of a separate colony, Upper Canada, in 1791.   It later became the province of Ontario. The motto of Ontario is Ut *incepit fidelis sic permanent* (Loyal she began and loyal she remains) which refers to the Loyalist refugees who arrived after the American Revolution.

It has been written about the Loyalists that up to July 4, 1776 and the Declaration of Independence the Loyalists:

"were every bit as American as their Whig (later known as Patriot) brethren. They feared social change and any increase in the power of the democratic element in society, but one looks in vain for Loyalists who were opposed to Liberty or the rights of Englishmen...The quarrel was over the mode of opposition; the Loyalists would not admit violence and believed the future of their country would be ruined by revolution and independence. It was not a case of colonial rights or 'passive obedience' but rather whether the colonies' future well-being could be best assured within the empire or without. The Loyalists had a fundamental trust in Britain, the Whigs (later called Patriots) a fundamental distrust." (4)

(4)"The King's Friends: The Composition and Motives of American Loyalist Claimants". By Wallace Brown, Providence, Rhode Island: Brown University Press, 1965.

In 1983 this envelope was issued to commemorate the bicentennial of the settlement of the Loyalists in Canada, formerly British North America.

Commemorative Envelope to mark Loyalist Bicentennial

The Canadian War Museum in marked the importance of this national bicentennial with a special travelling exhibition entitled The Loyal Americans. It indicated:

The impact of the settlement of the Loyalist political refugees in Canada was unique, profound, and permanent. There were close to 40,000 men, women and children who had suffered hardship and humiliation, endured a long, bitter war, and underwent immense material sacrifices in their attempt to preserve and defend the unity of the Empire. About 20,000 settled in Nova Scotia, 14,000 in what soon became New Brunswick, with smaller groups in Newfoundland, Saint John's (Prince Edward Island) and Cape Breton Island. Of the 6,000 or so Loyalists who sought refuge in the 'old province' of Quebec, some remained in the

established parts of the province, while the majority trekked to the unoccupied western portion of the province. This region subsequently became Upper Canada (Ontario).

Throughout British North America, the Loyalists contributed to the fashioning of a distinct and markedly different nation from the one they had been forced to flee. Their arrival and settlement produced an evolving federal concept based on the principle of two founding nations, the Loyalists and the French Canadians formed the warp and weft of the fundamental political and cultural fabric of Canadian life. In central Canada the Loyalists introduced such British political institutions as representative government, a constitutional cornerstone. In Atlantic Canada, parliamentary democracy based on a constitutional monarchy entrenched its British character. In Quebec, these political institutions proved both the inspiration and a powerful instrument for the achievement of 'survivance' for the Francophone population. These contributions will ensure the Loyalists will always remain an integral part of Canada's national heritage. (5)

(5)1783-1983 Loyalist Bicentennial Souvenir Envelope produced by Canadian War Museum for Bicentennial of the Settlement of the Loyalists in British North America

2. WHAT DOES THE UNITED EMPIRE LOYALISTS' ASSOCIATION OF CANADA DO?

All Branches of the United Empire Loyalists' Association of Canada (also referred to as the UELAC) are guided by a Mission Statement.

THE UNITED EMPIRE LOYALISTS' ASSOCIATION OF CANADA

MISSION STATEMENT

Our Mission is to preserve, promote and celebrate the history and traditions of the United Empire Loyalists.

We will accomplish our Mission by:

1) Uniting, in a Canadian-based association, descendants of families who remained loyal to the British crown during the American Revolutionary War, as well as persons interested in the Loyalist era and early Canadian history.

2) Supporting the collection and cataloguing of documents, books, artefacts, memorabilia and genealogical data relating to the United Empire Loyalists.

3) Facilitating and publishing research related to the United Empire Loyalists in the form of historical and family research journals, books, newsletters and digital media.

4) Providing Loyalist education resource materials and encouraging research through scholarship support.

5) Assisting in the construction and preservation of Loyalist monuments and memorials in Canada.

6) Participating in projects and activities which honour and celebrate the legacy of the United Empire Loyalists.

This mission statement was adopted at the Annual General Meeting May 30, 2015.
See: http://www.uelac.org/about.php#mission

The Hon. Alfred Gilpin Jones (1824 - 1896), born in Weymouth, Nova Scotia, son of Guy Carleton Jones, was the first President of the United Empire Loyalist Association of Nova Scotia founded in 1897. He also became a successful business person, politician, and public servant

Memorial Plaque to Hon. Alfred Gilpin Jones in St. Pa ul's Church, Halifax

In 1846 a Loyalist Refugee Association was formed in New Brunswick which may have been the earliest group to organize anywhere in Canada. The United Loyalist Society of New Brunswick was formed in 1883. This was the year of centennial celebrations for the Loyalist landing there.

16

The United Empire Loyalist Association of Quebec was formed in 1895 and the first meeting of a group in Ontario was held the next year.

Letters Patent incorporating the United Empire Loyalists; Association of Ontario were granted by the Province of Ontario on December 1, 1897. By its' constitution it provided for the formation of branches anywhere in Ontario. Membership was open to males who could trace descent from a United Empire Loyalist while spouses could become associate members. All applicants for membership were reviewed by an investigation committee which reported to a regular meeting of the Association. Candidates were declared elected members in consideration of the recommendation of the committee.

In 1912 it was moved at a meeting of the United Empire Loyalists' Association of Ontario that its' name be changed to the United Empire Loyalists' Association of Canada. Steps were then taken to incorporate as a national body and this was done through an Act of the Parliament of Canada in 1914. The Act permitted it to operate in all provinces and territories.

Toronto Branch was the first one to function and this continued for several years. In 1930 Loyalists throughout Canada were invited to join the Toronto Branch of the Association and advised that local branches would be established. At that time there were approximately 372 members.

Beginning in the 1930s branches were organized across Ontario in Brantford, Hamilton, Kingston, and Ottawa, as well as British Columbia, Manitoba and Saskatchewan.

The Nova Scotia Branch was granted its' Charter on March 8, 2014 by the United Empire Loyalists' Association of Canada.

The United Empire Loyalists' Association of Canada

To All and Every Member of

The United Empire Loyalists' Association of Canada

Know Ye that whereas by an Act passed by the Parliament of Canada, on the 27th day of May, in the year of our Lord, one thousand nine hundred and fourteen, and Chapter 146 of 4.5 George V 1914, the United Empire Loyalists' Association of Canada, hereinafter called "Association," became a body corporate and politic, with the powers in the said Act contained.

And Whereas a Petition has been presented to the said Association to grant a Warrant or Charter under the name of the Nova Scotia Branch, with its office or place of meeting at the Region of Halifax in the Province of Nova Scotia in Canada, and it is advisable to grant the Prayer of the said Petition, and to issue a Warrant for the institution of such Branch under the said Act, and the Constitution and By-Laws of the Association.

Now Know Ye that the petitioners are hereby constituted a Branch of the said Association under the title of the Nova Scotia Branch, to hold meetings at or near to the City of Halifax in the Province of Nova Scotia in Canada, with all the privileges and powers contained in the said Act and the By-Laws of the Association; subject to such provisos and conditions as are now or may hereafter be declared by the Constitution and By-Laws respecting the Association, and Branches thereof.

In Testimony Whereof the President and Secretary of the Association have hereunto set their hands, and the seal of the Association has been affixed, at Toronto, this 8th day of March in the year of our Lord, 2014.

The United Empire Loyalists' Association of Canada

Bonnie L. Schepers UE
President

Jo Ann M. Tuskin UE
Secretary

Nova Scotia Branch members have met for meetings around the province including in Digby, Upper Sackville, Shelburne, Tusket, Halifax, Port Mouton, Aylesford, Acaciaville, and as pictured below while attending a tour of the Old St. Edward's Loyalist Church and Museum in Upper Clements.

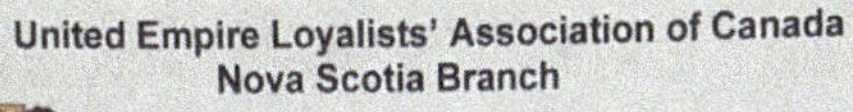

**United Empire Loyalists' Association of Canada
Nova Scotia Branch**

FALL MEETING !

WHEN: Saturday – September 22, 2018

WHERE: Acaciaville Baptist Church Hall
Acacia Valley Road, Acaciaville, NS

TIME : 11 a.m. – 12 Noon, Business Meeting
Lunch Break

1:30 – 3 p.m. Guest Speaker Allister Barton

In memory of his grandfather, the late Sgt. George William "Buster" Barton (1917-1995), Allister Barton has traced his family tree to the Black Pioneers, and the Black Loyalists of Brinley Town - a former Black settlement near Digby.
Join the journey of his Barton lineage and explore a 250 year old mystery that will bring Allister's family tree to life.

***All welcome to presentation by Guest Speaker
Bring a friend, a cousin, or grandparent***

For information email: novascotia@uelac.org

Nova Scotia Branch visit to Government House, Halifax

Members can submit their research and names of loyalist ancestors to help build the Online Loyalist Directory maintained by the United Empire Loyalists' Association. It now includes over 7,000 names. Since it has been estimated the number of Loyalists who came to Canada is many times that number it is a work in progress.

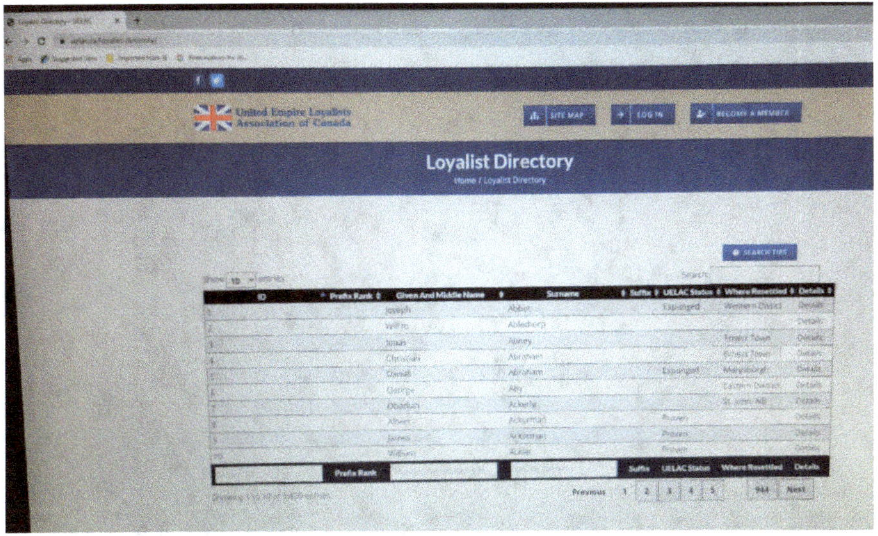

Online Loyalist Directory can be found at website of United Empire Loyalists"

Association of Canada at   https://uelac..ca

The Loyalist Gazette is published twice yearly by the United Empire Loyalists' Association of Canada and provided free to members. It contains articles of historical and genealogical information as well as news about Branch activities.

Providing Loyalist education resource materials and encouraging research through scholarship support is integral to the mission of the UELAC to preserve, promote and celebrate the history and traditions of the United Empire Loyalists. The Nova Scotia Branch supports these efforts and has been recognized for its' support of the Loyalist Scholarship Endowment Fund.

A National Conference is held in May or June each year where members from the Branches gather to attend genealogical and educational workshops, and take part in annual meeting. The location of the Conference is different each year and hosted by a local Branch. In 2018 it was held in Moose Jaw, Saskatchewan. In 2021 and 2022 the Conferences due to the Covid - 19 Coronavirus pandemic were arranged to be held virtually.

Dates & Locations of Recent National Conferences (2011 - 2021)

YEAR	LOCATION	HOST BRANCH(ES)
2021	Virtual (Cornwall, ON)	Bridge Annex
2020	Cancelled due to Covid – 19 Coronavirus	
2019	Gatineau, PQ	Sir Guy Carleton
2018	Moose Jaw, SASK	Saskatchewan
2017	London	London & W. ON / Grand River
2016	Summerside, PE	Abegweit / NS / NB
2015	Victoria, BC	Victoria
2014	Toronto, ON	Toronto
2013	Hamilton, ON	Hamilton
2012	Winnipeg, MAN	Manitoba
2011	Brockville, ON	Col. Edward Jessup

3. HOW TO OBTAIN A LOYALIST DESCENT 'UE' CERTIFICATE

In order to obtain a Loyalist Descent 'UE' Certificate you must first become a member of a Branch of the United Empire Loyalists' Association of Canada. There are branches across Canada and members can also join online. Membership is available whether you live within or outside Canada.

Application for Membership

Name _______________________________ Telephone (_____)_____________

Address ____

____

E-mail _____________________________ Date of birth _________________

Please select one: ▫ Individual membership   ▫ Student membership   ▫ Family membership   ▫ Institutional membership

Membership fees:

	Individual	Student	Family	Institutional
Full year	$50.00	$25.00	$70.00	$50.00
After 1 July	$25.00	$12.50	$35.00	$25.00

Student membership is available to full-time students under the age of 25.

If you have selected a family membership, please provide the names of other family members.

____

Please provide the following information for our files. Continue overleaf if necessary.

Name(s) of Loyalist Ancestor(s)	Where settled / Burial site

- Future dues notices should be sent by: ▫ E-mail   ▫ Regular Mail
- The Branch Newsletter should be sent by: ▫ E-mail   ▫ Regular Mail
- May we give your contact information to "distant cousins"?:   ▫ Yes   ▫ No

"Distant cousins" are persons who are researching ancestors that you may have in common.

Membership is handled by Branches only. Regular members are those who are interested in the aims and purposes of the Association, whether or not they are of Loyalist descent.

To receive a Certificate, which certifies your descent from a Loyalist Ancestor, the Certificate Application must be approved by the Genealogical Committee of the Dominion Council. The Certificate Application forms are available to members from the Branch.

Please make your cheque payable to the **Nova Scotia Branch, U.E.L. Association**) and mail it with this form to:

**The United Empire Loyalist Association of Canada
Nova Scotia Branch
PO Box 421
Halifax NS B3J 2P8
Canada**

Active Branches of UELAC & Year of Charter

<u>Maritimes</u>

New Brunswick, 1966 at Saint John

Nova Scotia, 2013

<u>Quebec</u>

Heritage, 1973 at Montreal

Little Forks, 1990

Sir John Johnson, 1967 at Cowansville

<u>Ontario</u>

Bay of Quinte Branch, 1956 met at Adolphustown

Bicentennial, 1984 at Windsor

Colonel John Butler, in 1934 called St. Catharines and District, changed name in 1992

Colonel Edward Jessup, 1968 at Prescott

Governor Simcoe, 1937 at Toronto

Grand River, formed in 1930s as Brantford, re – organized 1974

Hamilton, 1931

Kawartha, 1979

Kingston and District, 1932, however became inactive in 1937, new charter in 1979

London & Ontario West, 1973

Sir Guy Carleton, 1962 at Ottawa

St. Lawrence, 1934, inactive in late 1930s, reactivated 1977

Toronto, original in 1914; new charter in 1939

<u>Western Provinces</u>

Chilliwack, BC, 1990

Calgary, 1928

Edmonton, 1987

Manitoba,1933 called Winnipeg Branch, changed name in 1996

Saskatchewan, 1932, inactive at time of WWII, reactivated 1984

Thompson – Okanagan, 1995 at Vernon

Vancouver, original in 1932

Victoria, formed 1927, charter in 1940, lost, reactivated and new charter in 1969

<u>Virtual Branch</u>

Bridge Annex, 2018

Closed or Inactive Branches of UELAC & Year of Charter

<u>Maritimes</u>

Abegweit, 1973; (inactive)

Fredericton, 1975 ;(closed 2006)

Halifax – Dartmouth, 1979 ;(closed 2012/ formed Nova Scotia Branch)

Shelburne, 1975;(dissolved 1992)

Samuel Holland, 1973 at Saint John; (Closed 1975)

<u>Ontario</u>

Cornelius Thompson Branch, 1969 at Penetanguishene;(Closed)

Costume Branch, 1976;(Closed, 2005)

Governor Thomas Carleton, 1932; (Closed)

Upper Canada, 1985; (Closed 1994)

After you are a member of a Branch, if you are interested in proving descent from a United Empire Loyalist you will want to consider first who qualifies.

Who Qualifies as a Loyalist descendant?

General guidelines are:

(A) Either male or female, as of 19 April 1775, a resident of the American colonies, and joined the Royal Standard prior to the Treaty of Separation of 1783, or otherwise demonstrated loyalty to the Crown, and settled in territory remaining under the rule of the Crown; or

(B) a soldier who served in an American Loyalist Regiment and was disbanded in Canada; or

(C) member of the Six Nations of either the Grand River or the Bay of Quinte Reserve who is descended from one whose migration was similar to that of other Loyalists.

Being a proved Loyalist descendant confers no special status in Canadian or other society, but many members use the post-nominal letters "UE" after their name, in consequence of Lord Dorchester's Order in Council in 1789, conferring recognition of the service of the Loyalists in defense of "The Unity of Empire."

Source: http://www.uelac.org/membership.php

The Branch Genealogist and Assistant Genealogist can assist and guide you through the process of research.

WORKSHEET

Applicant Line of Descent From a Loyalist Ancestor

Loyalist Ancestor:					
Service to Crown:					
Loyalist Status by:					
Where & When Settled		Year & Loc. Born	Year & Loc. Married	Year & Loc. Died	CONNECTION and PROOF
Applicant	Name				
Parents	Father				
	Mother				
Grand Parents	Father				
	Mother				
1ˢᵗ Great Grand Parents	Father				
	Mother				
2ⁿᵈ Great Grand Parents	Father				
	Mother				
3ʳᵈ Great Grand Parents	Father				
	Mother				
4ᵗʰ Great Grand Parents	Father				
	Mother				
5ᵗʰ Great Grand Parents	Father				
	Mother				

As the Worksheet above indicates, you will need to obtain the information about all your ancestors going back to the United Empire Loyalist that you descend from.

Muster Rolls are one example of proof of Service to the Crown for a Loyalist. The Roll below shows a Company of King's Orange Rangers in 1777 stationed in New York.

Source: Library and Archives Canada, British Military Records

Another example of proof of service to the Crown can be a Petition by a Loyalist for land. The one below was made by Lieutenant John Cameron of the King's Orange Rangers in Sydney, Nova Scotia and accepted in 1797.

When you decide that you have completed your research and wish to submit an Application for a Loyalist Descent 'UE' Certificate you will provide the fee and the completed form.

The Application with your personal information includes choices about how you wish your Application processed. Your Branch Genealogist checks the form and it is provided to the Dominion Genealogists for review.

The Application asks you to list your ancestral lineage and proofs which will also be provided.

When your Application is approved by the Dominion Genealogists a Loyalist Descent "UE" Certificate will be sent to the Branch Genealogist for presentation, if possible.

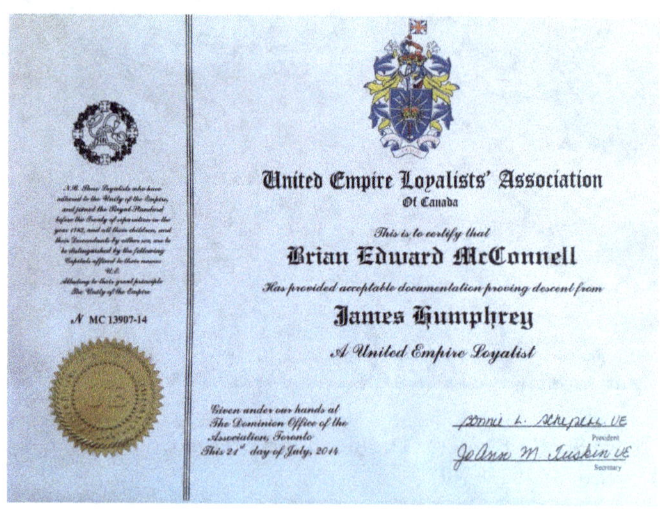

Certificate for United Empire Loyalist James Humphrey

The Loyalist Descent 'UE' Certificate includes Lord Dorchester's 1789 Proclamation, the Loyalist Badge, and the Armorial Bearings of the United Empire Loyalists' Association of Canada. It is signed by the President and Secretary of the Association.

Lord Dorchester, the Governor of Quebec, in a meeting of Council held on Monday, November 9, 1789 brought up the authority for the use of the letters U.E. Order of Council No. 24 was passed to place an honour on those families that had remained loyal during the American Revolution. It approved the use of the letters U.E. by Loyalist families and including the following:

"N.B. Those Loyalists who have adhered to the unity of the Empire, and joined the Royal Standard before the Treaty of Separation in the year 1783, and all their children and their descendants by either sex, are to be distinguished by the following capitals affixed to their names: U.E. alluding to their great principle the unity of the Empire."

In a covering letter which Lord Dorchester sent with the Order to London, he explained: "Care had been taken to reward the spirit of loyalty and industry, to extend and transmit it to future generations."

In 1897, The United Empire Loyalist Association of Ontario, predecessor to the United Empire Loyalists' Association of Canada, was led by George Sterling Ryerson, physician, teacher, militia and army officer, politician, author, and businessman As President he decided to secure official authorization for a special badge and insignia.

"In 1897 the Association sent a petition to the Queen requesting royal sanction. Pointing out that 'it was the intention of Her Majesty's Royal

Predecessor, George III, that the Petitioners Ancestors and their descendants should be accorded a special mark of honour of a permanent and enduring character whereby they should at all times be distinguished from other settlers in Canada,'
the association suggested that the queen's jubilee 'should be the occasion of the more complete carrying out of His late Majesty's intention and be marked by the conferring upon the Petitioners and those whom they represent a further and more enduring mark of honour." (7)

Ryerson travelled to England and attempted to meet with the British Prime Minister. He was unsuccessful in seeing him but did meet with his under- secretary who indicated he had never heard of the Loyalists and could not see any reason why the state should acknowledge their existence. Further to this the Colonial Office contacted the Governor General of Canada, Lord Aberdeen, to determine the position of Canadian Prime Minister Wilfred Laurier.

Apparently sensitive to anti-imperialist sentiment in his native province of Quebec, Laurier advised any action on the matter would have to wait until a 'more propitious season.' The colonial secretary, Lewis Harcourt, informed Ryerson that to revive a colonial order - in – council that had been dormant for more than a century would be 'impolitic'.
It was made clear to Ryerson that the British Colonial Office would not authorize the Association's badge without prior approval of the Canadian government. Nonetheless, he was not dismayed in his support for the Loyalist heritage and continued to be active. Letters Patent incorporating the United Empire Loyalists' Association of Ontario were granted by the Province of Ontario on December 1, 1897. Ryerson was the first President of the Association. He is also known as the founder of the Canadian branch of the Red Cross. (8)

(7) Knowles, Norman, "Inventing the Loyalists - The Ontario Loyalist Tradition & the Creation of Usable Pasts", University of Toronto Press, 1997, page 153.

(8) "Loyally Yours - 100 Years of the UELAC", compiled by Frederick H. Hayward and printed by Global Genealogy.com Inc.,2014

Over the years as there have been political changes in Canada the United Empire Loyalists' Association of Canada has evolved as can be seen by changes in the purposes of the Association. Describing what is important to recognizing the Loyalist heritage has changed. The concept of Unity of The Empire which the letters U.E. referred to and associated loyalty to the Crown was included in the language of the Association when it was founded.

The United Empire Loyalists of Ontario became incorporated on May 27, 1914 in a statute of the Dominion of Canada and changed its' name to "The United Empire Loyalists' Association of Canada". (9) Its' connection to the former British Empire was well noted as its' first purpose included "to perpetuate this spirit of loyalty to the Empire".

There were five purposes being:

(a) to united together irrespective of creed or political party, the descendants of those families who, during the American revolutionary war of 1775 to 1783, sacrificed their homes in retaining their loyalty to the British Crown, and to perpetuate the spirit of loyalty to the Empire;

(9) "The Law Times", Vol. 138, March 13, 1915, p. 443

(b) to preserve the history and traditions of that important epoch in Canadian history by rescuing from oblivion the history and traditions of the loyalist families before it is too late;

(c) to collect together in a suitable place the portraits, documents, books, weapons, flags, monuments, memorials, and all other articles relating to the United Empire Loyalists which are now scattered throughout Canada and elsewhere;

(d) to publish an historical and genealogical journal or annual transactions;

(e) to erect, construct, and repair buildings, monuments, memorials, and also to purchase real estate and other things that may be considered desirable to perpetuate the memory of the United Empire Loyalists.

The stated purposes of the United Empire Loyalists Association of Canada have gone through a number of changes. By 2002, with the passing of the British Empire and its replacement by the Commonwealth the reference to 'loyalty to the Empire' was removed. (10)

(10) Mission Statement of United Empire Loyalists' Association of Canada adopted at the Annual General Meeting June 8, 2002

The sixth item in the mission statement included "defending and promoting... the Constitutional Monarchy, the Commonwealth..." The entire mission statement was:

"To preserve, promote and celebrate the history and traditions of the Loyalist epoch in Canadian history by:

1)Uniting in a Canadian association the descendants of those families who, during the American Revolutionary War, sacrificed all to retain their loyalty to the British crown.

2) Collecting and cataloguing portraits, documents, books, weapons, flags, clothing and other artifacts relating to the United Empire Loyalists.

3) Publishing an historical and family research journal, books and newsletters as well as educational resource materials and encouraging scholarship and publication about Loyalist history and demography.

4) Erecting, constructing and repairing buildings, monuments and memorials in Canada to perpetuate the memory of the United Empire Loyalists.

5) Increasing public awareness of the Loyalist contributions to Canada and preserving, defending, and promoting Loyalist heritage within Canadian society, by developing and participating in projects and activities which honour and celebrate the memory of the United Empire Loyalists.

6) Defending and promoting the values and institutions fundamental to Canada's United Empire Loyalist heritage and, in

particular, the Constitutional Monarchy, the Commonwealth, Parliamentary Government, the Rule of Law, Human Rights and Unity."

The most dramatic change in the purpose of the United Empire Loyalists' Association of Canada appeared in 2015 with the removal of support and promotion of the Constitutional Monarchy and Commonwealth. (11) The current mission statement adopted also now includes new wording that specifically includes support for collecting genealogical data in Item 2 and in Item 4 provides for encouraging research through scholarship support. It reads:

**"Our Mission is to preserve, promote and celebrate the history and traditions of the United Empire Loyalists.
We will accomplish our Mission by:**

1) Uniting, in a Canadian-based association, descendants of families who remained loyal to the British crown during the American Revolutionary War, as well as persons interested in the Loyalist era and early Canadian history.

2) Supporting the collection and cataloguing of documents, books, artefacts, memorabilia and genealogical data relating to the United Empire Loyalists.

3) Facilitating and publishing research related to the United Empire Loyalists in the form of historical and family research journals, books, newsletters and digital media.

4) Providing Loyalist education resource materials and encouraging research through scholarship support.
5) Assisting in the construction and preservation of Loyalist monuments and memorials in Canada.

6) Participating in projects and activities which honour and celebrate the legacy of the United Empire Loyalists."

(11) Mission Statement of United Empire Loyalists' Association of Canada adopted at the Annual General Meeting May 30, 2015.

The recognition of the importance of genealogical data also is reflective of another change which occurred. Originally to become a member of the Association required simply a form signed by two existing members who vouched for you as a descendant of a United Empire Loyalist. However, now and for many years Branches of the Association have genealogists who review detailed forms and there are Dominion Genealogists who review applications.

The plate pictured on following page shows the badge of the United Empire Loyalists' Association of Canada. It proclaims enduring loyalty to the Crown with the words "Loyal Then - Loyal Now". The badge consists of a wreath made up of red maple leaves and oak leaves and acorns. The maple leaves represent Canada while the oak leaves and acorns are a long - held symbol of loyalty and fidelity to the monarchy. In the centre is the Cypher G III R, signifying Georgius Tertius Rex, the sovereign to whom the Loyalists gave their devotion and their service. It along with the Coat of Arms were approved at a time when the stated purpose of the Association included loyalty to the Empire as described in an article in 1972 by Conrad Swan, York Herald of Arms-in-Ordinary to Her Majesty The Queen and Honorary Vice-President, UELAC. (12)

(12) "The Armorial Bearings of The United Empire Loyalists' Association Of Canada" by Conrad Swan, Loyalist Gazette, Vol. X, No. 2, Autumn, 1972

Plate with Badge of Member of United Empire Loyalists'

Association of Canada

Today use of the initials is not common place but is still used by some who have become aware of their Loyalist heritage and wish to confirm their ancestral connection. Perhaps two of the most prominent Canadians to use it in recent times have been Rt. Hon. Ellen Louks Fairclough P.C., D.C. , F.C.A., L.L.D. F.R.C.G.S., D.H. U.E. and The Honourable Peter Andrew Stewart Milliken, P.C, U.E, B.A., M.A, LL.B

Fairclough was a Chartered Accountant who served on the city council of Hamilton, Ontario for five years before being elected to the Canadian House of Commons from 1950 - 1963. She advocated women's rights including equal pay for equal work and while in government was chosen the first female member of the Cabinet.

Peter Milliken graduated from Queen's University, Dalhousie University, and Oxford before becoming a lawyer in Kingston, Ontario. He was elected Member of Parliament from Kingston and the Islands in 1985 and served until his retirement in 2011. In 2001 he was elected Speaker of the House of Commons and held that position until he retired in 2011. His Loyalists ancestors came from the Mohawk Valley of New York State. He is an Honorary President of the United Empire Loyalists' Association of Canada.

Recognition of Loyalist roots includes many things in addition to knowing the history of the postnominal UE. Several provinces and cities have designated a 'Loyalist Day' as recognition of the importance the more than 50,000 Loyalists who came to Canada as refugees played in the development of the country. They were the first large influx of multi-ethnic immigrants. It is an opportunity for those of Loyalist heritage as well as other Canadians to take time to appreciate this past.

There is no special place today according to the Canadian government for those who bear the UE designation. This is partly because during the past 100 years Canada has moved away from recognizing hereditary honours. In 1919, the House of Commons passed the so-called 'Nickle Resolution' which directed the practice of bestowing titles of honour by foreign governments on Canadians be discontinued. There was a brief revival of the foreign honours system during the administration of Prime Minister R. B. Bennet and several knighthoods and lesser distinctions were awarded in 1934-5.

In 1968 the government published "regulations respecting the acceptance and wearing by Canadians of Commonwealth and foreign orders, decorations and medals", and in 1988 it adopted a resolution that declared the Canadian government would not approve an order or decoration that carries with it a title of honour or any implication of precedence or privilege..."

A letter from an official with an office of the Canadian government that refers to the letters UE was posted on the internet group Rootsweb regarding the Subject: Post-Nominal Letters on September 17, 1999. It stated:

Dear Mr. Eamer:

Thank you for your email dated September 7, 1999, regarding post-nominal letters UE.

The designation UE never has been part of the national honours system in Canada. As you are aware, the designation was proposed in late 1789 as a mark of honour by Lord Dorchester, then Governor-in-Chief of Quebec. It was proposed to be borne by Loyalists and their descendants. The use of the mark of honour was never made official by King George III, but the initial UE rapidly came to be used as an administrative convenience, to ensure that Loyalists and their descendants enjoyed certain privileges when receiving grants for Crown lands.

Had George III, or one of his successors, subsequently made the designation an official one, it would now contravene national honours policy, which does not provide for hereditary honours of this type. In these circumstances, the genealogical registries kept by the United Empire Loyalist Association of Canada and the procedures which support their creation and maintenance probably offers the best approach for preservation of the Loyalist heritage in a particular family. You may also wish to petition for a coat-or-arms, which, if granted, can include elements honouring a Loyalist heritage. You may forward your request at the following address:

The Canadian Heraldic Authority

The Chancellery, Rideau Hall

1 Sussex Drive

Ottawa, Canada K1A 0A1

Yours sincerely,

Marie - Paule Thorn, Honours Information Officer

The UE initials were begun by Lord Dorchester when he was Governor of Quebec in 1789 and it was instituted in the documents of the day. (13)

(13) For further information on Lord Dorchester's Resolution see "United Empire Loyalists – A Guide to Tracing Loyalist Ancestors in Upper Canada" by Brenda Dougall Merriman, Global Heritage Press, 2006

4. LOYALIST DESCENT 'UE' CERTIFICATES PRESENTED IN ATLANTIC CANADA

This is a partial listing to provide an illustration of the United Empire Loyalists who have been confirmed for Certificates by the United Empire Loyalists' Association of Canada.   After each name is some identifying information followed by the Branch which the most recent application was made through and the year of certification.

A

Acorn, John – born in Broad Bay, Maine in 1761.
Joined in 3rd Regiment of Rangers and came to Prince Edward Island in 1782.   Died July 3, 1857 at age of 96. (Abegweit, 1996)

Allen, Jeremiah – born in Beverly, Essex Co., Massachusetts. Died April 6, 1809 and buried in Saint George's Anglican Church Cemetery in Sydney, Nova Scotia (Nova Scotia, 2018)

Anderson, Thomas - born December 25,1745 in Fairfield County Connecticut. Served in New York Volunteers.   Came to Granville, Nova Scotia in 1783 where built home at Karsdale. Died June 13, 1809 and buried in Christ Church Anglican Cemetery. (Nova Scotia, 2018)

**Christ Church Anglican Church built by United Empire Loyalists completed
in 1791 at Karsdale, Annapolis County, Nova Scotia**

Anderson, Peter - born about 1723.   In 1782, he was a loyalist
associator at New York. He left about 1783, perhaps at the time loyalist
forces were evacuated, to settle in Shelburne, Nova Scotia. In 1785, he
received grants of land at Parr Town (Now part of Saint John) in New
Brunswick and also in Sunbury County near Grand Lake. Died on Nov
13, 1828 in Fredericton, New Brunswick at the age of 95. (Halifax –
Dartmouth, 1994)

Appleby, John - born in 1762 from Bergen County, New Jersey. Served with New Jersey Volunteers. Died December 19, 1825 and buried in Chocolate Cove Cemetery, Charlotte County, New Brunswick. (Vancouver, 2010)

Autrey, Absolum - born in North Carolina. Listed as a Tory officer in the Revolutionary War on page 196, Vol 22, of "The Colonial Records of North Carolina" (Halifax – Dartmouth, 2012)

Atwater, William - born in New Haven, Connecticut in 1759. Settled in Guysborough, Nova Scotia. Died there July 21, 1845.   (Victoria, 2021)

B

Babbit, Daniel – born April 27, 1742 in New Miford, New Haven, Connecticut. Went to New Brunswick in 1783.   Worked as blacksmith in Gagetown. Died July 12, 1830 in Gagetown, New Brunswick (Heritage, 2018)

Balmain, William - born in Scotland and came to America in 1773. Went to Saint John, New Brunswick in 1783 Settled in Scotchtown, New Brunswick. Died in Saint John, New Brunswick in 1809. (Victoria, 2008)

Bangs, Seth – born 14 July 1738 at Harwich, Barnstable, Massachusetts. Served throughout the Revolutionary War as a pilot for the British

Navy, consequently his Massachusetts property was confiscated and sold in 1778 and he was specifically named in the "Banishment Act of the State of Massachusetts". Went to Nova Scotia likely some time between the evacuation of Boston by the British and Loyalists in March 1776 and his being proscribed in 1778. In 1784 received land grant of 200 acres in Chester, Nova Scotia. (Nova Scotia, 2021)

Barberie, Captain John -   Captain in New Jersey Volunteers, Went to Saint John, New Brunswick after American Revolution. Died 1818 in Sussex Corner, Kings County, New Brunswick. (Kawartha, 2010)

Bayard, Samuel Vetch - Major in the King's Orange Rangers. Land Grant of 4730 acres at Aylesford, Nova Scotia which sold and purchased 5,000 acres at Wilmot. Family donated church bell for Holy Trinity Anglican Church in Middleton. Died in 1832 and buried in Family plot on his land at South Farmington.   (Nova Scotia, 2020)

Baxter, Captain Simon – born in 1730 in Holland County, Connecticut. Died March 20, 1804 and buried in Big Rock Cemetery at Bloomfield, Kings County, New Brunswick.   (Kawartha, 2012)

Bessonett, Capt. Daniel – from Bristol, Pennsylvania. Captain in 4th Battalion, New Jersey Volunteers. Died in Halifax, Nova Scotia. (Nova Scotia,.2019)

Blakley, Chambers – born in about 1749 in County Down, Northern Ireland. In 1767 sailed from Belfast to take up land in South Carolina. Served in loyalist militia. Evacuated from Charleston on ship "Argo" for Halifax in 1782. Took up land grant at Ship Harbour. (Halifax - Dartmouth,1996)

Blois, Abraham – born in 1744 in Essex, England. He came to America on board the sailing ship Peggy as an indentured husbandman. The Peggy sailed from London, England the week of January 15, 1774 bound for Baltimore, Maryland. Abraham fought for both the Americans and the British in the Revolutionary War. As a Loyalist, he took up land in Nova Scotia after the war. Died January 25, 1839 and buried with headstone in the Blois Family Cemetery at Gore, Hants County, Nova Scotia. (Nova Scotia, 2016)

Bonnell, Benjamin –   born in Morris County, New Jersey in 1744. Served in Loyal American Legion. Went to Saint John, New Brunswick in 1783. Granted land at Long Reach, Kings County. Died February 19, 1828. (Heritage, 2020)

Bower, Adam - Johann Adam Bauer (later Adam Bower) was born November 13, 1724 in Hottenbach, Rheinland, Germany. Emigrated in 1764 and settled in South Carolina. Joined the British Army in Augusta during the American Revolution, serving in Captain Maxwell's

Company. In September 1782, when the British were forced to evacuate Charleston, Adam moved his family to Nova Scotia. They wintered that year in Halifax with several other Loyalist families, and in July 1783 arrived in Port Roseway, and at Shelburne, Nova Scotia, May 17, 1783   Died 1801. (Halifax, 1989)

Bower, Charles – son of Adam Bower. Also joined British Army and came to Shelburne, Nova Scotia after war. (Nova Scotia, 2021)

Bowlby, Richard – born 1718 in Mansfield, Woodhouse, Nottingham County, England. He came with his parents while a young man to America. Lived at Mansfield Township, Sussex County, New Jersey and was a Justice of the Peace for County. During the American Revolution, he was a Loyalist and went to the British lines in New York. In 1779, his lands in Sussex County were confiscated by the Rebels. Following the war he went in the 1783 Loyalist exodus from New York to Nova Scotia and settled at Digby Township., Nova Scotia. Died 1818. (Shelburne, 1983)

Braddock, Samuel – served in 1st Battalion of King's Rangers. Disbanded in fall of 1783 at Charlottetown, Prince Edward Island (Abegweit, 1999)

Brittain, Joseph - born September 24, 1759 in Middletown, Monmouth, New Jersey. Served as Private, and from October 1782, then as Ensign in the 1st Battalion, New Jersey Volunteers. He went to New Brunswick after the war. Died on May 26, 1830 in King's County, New Brunswick. (Nova Scotia, 2015)

Brooks, Abraham – from New Jersey, born about 1760. Served in the New Jersey Volunteers which was organized with citizens of Essex County, New Jersey in the 1780s. Received grant of 200 acres in Digby Township, Nova Scotia as Loyalist. Died at Weymouth, Nova Scotia in 1830. (Nova Scotia, 2017)

Brunson, Daniel – born November 13, 1757 in Kent, Litchfield County, Connecticut. Served as Ensign in Prince of Wales American Regiment. Settled in St. Mary's Parish, York County, New Brunswick. Relocated to Eastern Townships of Quebec. (Nova Scotia, 2021)

Buckman, Samuel - born in Boston, Suffolk, Massachusetts on February 16, 1763. Died September 24, 1853 in Westport, Brier Island, Digby County, Nova Scotia. (Nova Scotia, 2021)

Burhoe, John – born February 2, 1756 on Channel Islands, Guernsey. Served as Private with Royal Nova Scotia Regiment. Settled at Alexandra, Prince Edward Island. (Vancouver, 2012)

Burlock, Job – born in Lancashire, England on May 5, 1730. Resided in Wilton, Fairfield County, Connecticut. (Halifax - Dartmouth 1996)

C

Campbell, Colin – born in Inverary, Scotland about 1751. Lawyer. Came to New York and in 1783 with other Loyalists to Shelburne. Served as representative to Nova Scotia Assembly and collector of customs. Moved to Weymouth and died July 30, 1835. Buried in St. Peter's Anglican Church Cemetery at Weymouth North. (Shelburne, 1981)

Chandler, Joshua - born at Woodstock, Connecticut on March 1, 1727. Graduated from Yale in Law. Appointed Justice of the Peace in 1769, served New Haven, Connecticut as a selectman, and member of the General Assembly May 1768-72, 1774 and 1775. In 1775, when his Loyalist sympathies became evident, he was placed under guard in North Haven. In 1779, son William aided a British invasion on New Haven, and the family withdrew with the British, forfeiting Joshua's property. In autumn of 1782, accepted appointment as Agent for the Settlers in Nova Scotia for the loyalist refugees of Long Island's Queens County. Joshua's wife Sarah (Miles) Chandler died only weeks after arriving in Annapolis. In 1784, Joshua made trip to England to sue for compensation for his losses. In March 1787, granted an 1800-acre grant of land in Digby (at the mouth of the Annapolis River basin) as well as 300 acres in Clements, a settlement ten miles up the Annapolis River, and sailed for Saint John, New Brunswick where the Commissioners were hearing claims. Travelled with son William and daughter Elizabeth. Schooner went aground and William was drowned in the wreck, Joshua died in a fall from a rocky point while searching for help, and daughter Elizabeth, and another woman, died from exposure Bodies buried in Fernhill Cemetery in Saint John. Inscription on the gravestone reads *Here lyeth the Bodies of Col. Joshua Chandler, Aged 61 years and William Chandler His Son Aged 29 years, who*
were Ship wreck'd on their passage from Digby to St. John on the night of the 9th day of March 1787 & perished in the Woods on the 11th of said Month. and *Here lyeth the Bodies of Mrs. Sarah Grant Aged 38 Years Widow of the late Major Alex Grant; & Miss Elizabeth Chandler aged 27 years, who were Shipwreck'd on their passage from Digby to St. John on the Night of the 9th day of*

March 1787 and Perished in the Woods on the 11th of said Month. (Nova Scotia, 2019)

Chase, James - born in 1744 in Freetown, Bristol County, Massachusetts. Joined the British Army in 1778 at Rhode Island. He died September 23, 1816 at his farm in Burton, Sunbury County, New Brunswick and is buried in Burton Parish. (Nova Scotia, 2018)

Church, Charles - born May 22, 1740 in Freetown, Bristol, Massachusetts Bay. With family of eleven persons, and three servants, he went from New York to Shelburne, Nova Scotia, where granted one town and one water lot. (Nova Scotia, 2016)

Colter, William – born in Donegal, Ireland. Served in 84th Regiment of Foot. Settled on lands in Douglas Township, Hants County, Nova Scotia (Nova Scotia, 2020)

Cowperthwaite, Hugh – born in Salem County, New Jersey in 1733. Came to New Brunswick in 1783 and first settled in Sheffield Parish, Sunbury County, then moved to Waterborough Parish, Queens County. Died November 2, 1828. (Victoria, 2011)

Craig, Private John – born in Scotland about 1750. Served in 84th Regiment of Foot. Died in 1833 and buried in Second Falls United Baptist Cemetery in Charlotte County, New Brunswick (Fredericton, 1984)

U.E. Loyalist marker for Private John Craig on gravestone in Second Falls United Baptist Church Cemetery in Second Falls, Charlotte County, New Brunswick

Craig, James -   born about 1755 in Suffolk County, New York. Served in DeLanceys Brigade. Settled in Carleton County, New Brunswick (Victoria, 2020)

Crawford, Edward – born on Isle of Skye, Scotland and moved to Carolina in 1752. Served in Loyalist militia. Came to Nova Scotia with wife and received 500 acres in Chezzetcook – Lawrencetown area. (Nova Scotia, 2021)

Crawford, James -   born in Pound Ridge, New York on April 13, 1743. Joined the Guides and Pioneers. In 1783 went to New Brunswick and settled on Long Reach, Kings County. Died May 8, 1830 and buried behind Trinity Anglican Church in Kingston, New Brunswick. (Grand River, 1980)

Crowder, William - born about 1730 and moved from Virginia to Kinderhook, New York, where he married Hannah Rous about 1748. He served with the British army during the French and Indian War, and also during the Revolutionary War, and in 1778 his family arrived seeking refuge to join him with the British forces near Kingston, Ontario. The family later settled on land in Osnabruck Township, Stormont County, Ontario. (Nova Scotia, 2020)

Crowe, Richard Robert - born in Galway, Ireland. Commanded a company of Black Pioneers during the American Revolution. After war he was granted lands in Parrsborough Township, Kings County (now Cumberland, Nova Scotia. (Certificate granted 2017)

Crowell, Captain Joseph – Resident of Middletown, Monmouth County, New Jersey. Captain in 5th Battalion and later 1st Battalion, New Jersey Volunteers. Settled in Carleton, New Brunswick. (Nova Scotia, 2014)

Currie, Joshua - born in about December, 1741 at Cortlandtown, Westchester County New York. Served with Loyal American Regiment. In the fall of 1783, Joshua and his family evacuated with the British forces to the St. John River Valley and received a land grant upriver around Gagetown, New Brunswick. Died at age 60 on 20 September 1802 and buried in Chase Cemetery, Gagetown, New Brunswick, Canada. Died September 20, 1802. (Col. John Butler, 2019)

Cutler, Ebenezer - born on July 10, 1740. Sutton, Worcester, Massachusetts. In 1776, he went with the British army to Halifax. He was proscribed and banished in 1778, settled in Nova Scotia, and was Prothonotary of the County of Annapolis. (Nova Scotia, 2015)

D

Darby, Benjamin – native of Devonshire, England, born June, 1744. Emigrated to Rhode Island. Served throughout the American Revolution as a scout in Rogers Rangers. Died March 3, 1844 and buried in Saint John's Church Anglican Cemetery in St. Eleanor's, Prince Edward Island. (Abegweit, 2017)

Day, John –   born about 1740 in New Jersey. Served with 2nd Battalion, New Jersey Volunteers. Settled in Queens County, New Brunswick (Victoria, 2009)

Denton, Joseph Sr.- born in 1752 in Huntington, Suffolk, New York. He arrived as a Loyalist in 1784 in Nova Scotia, having sailed from Long Island on the ship Atalanta. He appears on the 1784 muster roll of the town of Digby with 5 members of his family. In 1801 he was granted 210 acres in Digby Township. (Nova Scotia, 2020).

Dibblee, Fyler –   born on January 18, 1741 in Stamford, Fairfield County, New Brunswick. Died May 6, 1784 at Woodstock, Carleton County, New Brunswick.   (Governor Simcoe, 2011)

Dickie, Hector - came to South Carolina from Belfast, Northern Ireland in 1768. Lieutenant and later Captain in Colonel John Cotton's Regiment, Steven's Creek Militia, Ninety - Six Brigade, South Carolina. Died on April 27, 1837 and buried in Norton, King's County, New Brunswick. (Hamilton, 2010)

Ditmars, Douwe, - born at Jamaica, Queen's, New York in 1723. Arrived in Nova Scotia from New York in the fall of 1783. He settled at Clements Township.   Founder of Clementsport.   Donated land and wood for Old St. Edward's Anglican Church. Died in 1796. (Nova Scotia, 2020)

Douwe Ditmars Headstone in Old St. Edward's Church Cemetery

Dotten, James, Sr. - - from Westchester, New York settled at Wallace, Cumberland County, Nova Scotia. (Nova Scotia, 2015)

Dykeman, Garrett - from White Plains, Westchester County, New York. Born March 4, 1741. Died June 20, 1813 and buried in Saint John's Anglican Church Cemetery at Gagetown, New Brunswick. (New Brunswick, 2006)

E

Earle, Justus – born August 19, 1749 in Bergen County, New Jersey and served in 4th Battalion, New Jersey Volunteers. Died September 22, 1826 in Grande Point, Queens County, New Brunswick. (New Brunswick, 2012)

Edgett, Joel - born in 1761 in Westchester County, New York.   In 1783 came to New Brunswick. Settled Edgett's Landing, New Brunswick (Victoria, 2017)

Embree, Joseph – in 1784 came to Cumberland County, Nova Scotia from Westchester County, New York. Was Private in Loyalist militia during American Revolution. Granted 500 acres. Died November 18, 1828 and buried in Embree Cemetery in Rose, Cumberland County, Nova Scotia at age 68. (Halifax - Dartmouth, 1983)

Headstone for Joseph Embree & wife Catherine in Embree Cemetery

Embree, Lieutenant Samuel – born in 1746 in Westchester County, New York. Served with DeLanceys Brigade as Lieutenant. Settled in Cumberland County, Nova Scotia. Died 1800 in Amherst, Nova Scotia. (Victoria, 2019)

Ensor, George – from Pennsylvania. Went to Shelburne, Nova Scotia. Died 1805 (Nova Scotia, 2016)

Etter, Benjamin - watchmaker, silversmith, office holder, militia officer, and shipowner; b. 1763 in Braintree, Massachusetts. Benjamin Etter's father emigrated to the Thirteen Colonies from Bern, Switzerland, in 1737, settling first in Philadelphia and later, in 1752, in Braintree, where he earned his living as a weaver. Peter Etter remained loyal to the crown after the outbreak of the Revolutionary War, and with the evacuation of Boston in March 1776 he and his family of seven left Boston for Halifax in one of the transports carrying troops and civilian refugees. By 1780 Benjamin was working in Halifax as an apprentice with his elder brother Peter, a watchmaker. In 1784 he received a grant of 100 acres in Chester Township, but since he failed to improve the land it was escheated in 1811. Peter Jr, who had served at Fort Cumberland (near Sackville, N.B.) as a sergeant in Lieutenant-Colonel Joseph Gorhams Royal Fencible Americans during the abortive uprising of Jonathan Eddy in 1776, left Halifax in 1787 to establish a business in Westmorland County, N.B. Benjamin was placed in charge of the Halifax shop but, as he had completed his apprenticeship, he soon began working independently as a watchmaker in a shop on Hollis Street. (Nova Scotia, 2019)

Etter, Peter - born 1715 in Switzerland. Moved to Philadelphia, Pennsylvania and then to Boston. See Benjamin Etter above. Evacuated to Halifax, Nova Scotia in 1786. Died June 24, 1794 in Halifax, Nova Scotia (Victoria, 2016)

Ettinger, Lewis - born in Germany. Enlisted in American militia, Captured. Joined 84th Regiment of Foot.   Grant of 500 acres as part of Major John Small's Loyalists Grant for troops of 84th as a Sergeant's entitlement in Hants County, Nova Scotia. (Halifax, 2016)

Road sign for Ettinger Road in Upper Kennetcook, Hants Co., Nova Scotia

F

Fenton, Jacob – Sergeant in King's Rangers in Carolina. Came to Nova Scotia and settled at East Country Harbour. (Shelburne, 1979)

Fowler, Henry – born in 1756 in Westchester County, New York. Died February 2, 1843 and buried in Acadian Loyalist Cemetery at French Village, Kings County, New Brunswick. (Vancouver, 1989)

G

Ganong, Thomas – from Mahopac, Putnam County, New York. Died

April 20, 1810 and buried in Trinity Anglican Cemetery at Kingston, Kings County, New Brunswick (New Brunswick, 2005)

Gates, Oldham – born in Norfolk, Massachusetts in 1716, Settled in Annapolis where was shipbuilder. (Nova Scotia, 2019)

Gavel, John Sr. – born about 1745 in Brookhaven, Suffolk, New York. Granted 200 acres on Tusket River, Yarmouth County. Nova Scotia. Died about 1809 in Gavelton, Yarmouth County, Nova Scotia. (Halifax – Dartmouth, 2012)

Gavelton Meeting House in area settled in 1784 by United Empire Loyalists is only remaining New England Style meeting house in Yarmouth County, Nova Scotia

Gesner, Henry – born on November 10, 1756 in Tappan, Rockland, New York. Served in King's Orange Rangers. Died on October 13, 1850 at Cornwallis Township, Kings County, Nova Scotia (Nova Scotia, 2017)

Gidney, Joshua - born in 1733 in Westchester County, New York. Settled at Grand Lake, Queens County, New Brunswick. Died July 24, 1819 in Waterborough Parish, Queens County, New Brunswick. (Victoria, 2016)

Golding, John - born 1736 in Westchester County, New York. Served in DeLanceys Brigade. Settled in Queens County, New Brunswick (Victoria, 2008)

Gray, Jesse - Jesse and brother Samuel joined the Loyalist cause during the American Revolution. They were in Captain Daniel Plumber's Company of the Ninety-Six Brigade of North Carolina. At the Loyalist surrender there, Jesse and Samuel (Samuel is mentioned in "The Loyalists of East Florida" by Wilber Siefert) made their way to St Johns Bluffs, near Jacksonville, Fla. At the end of hostilities, Samuel stayed in the new United States while Jesse left from St. Augustine, Fla for Shelburne, Nova Scotia. (Nova Scotia, 2018)

H

Hamilton, James - born March 2, 1735 in Hamilton, Lanarkshire, Scotland. Died before September 9, 1823 in Middle Clyde, Shelburne, Nova Scotia. In about 1773 James & Anna Hamilton and their infant daughter, Margaret, sailed from Scotland to the British colony of New York and settled near the Hudson River in Newburgh, Ulster

(Orange)County, New York. Went to Shelburne, Nova Scotia in 1783. While in Shelburne he was commander of the Port Roseway military district and a prominent citizen. He was granted 450 acres of land for his military service. (Nova Scotia, 2018).

Hankinson, Reuben – born February 28, 1758 in Shrewsbury, Monmouth County, New Jersey. Served in New Jersey Volunteers. Settled after war along Sissiboo River in Weymouth, Nova Scotia. (Halifax – Dartmouth, 2005)

Harding, Lieut. Israel – born in Rhode Island. During the American Revolution, Israel became active as a civilian, providing information and supplies to the English. As a result of these activities, his land in Connecticut was confiscated by the Revolutionary Government, and he and his family removed to New York, and then to Nova Scotia. (Halifax – Dartmouth, 2012)

Hart, Josiah - born in Wallingford, Connecticut in 1741. Following the American Revolution, he and his family "removed to Nova Scotia", and were among the "Associated Loyalists of Connecticut" who obtained a grant of land to settle at Manchester Township, Guysborough County. (Nova Scotia, 2021)

Hatfield, Captain John - Captain of 3rd New Jersey Volunteers during American Revolution. Came to Nova Scotia as United Empire Loyalist. Born in Dorset, England. About 1740. Died November 16, 1804 in Fox River, Cumberland County, Nova Scotia. (Halifax – Dartmouth, 2006)

Heartz, John - born in Holland about 1735.Went to New York. In 1776 in New York Gazette name listed as signer of Declaration of Allegiance to King George III. To Shelburne in 1783 and then to Prince Edward Island about 1786. (Abegweit, 1973)

Hierlihy, Philip – born about 1755 in Ireland. Served with Prince of

Wales American Regiment. Settled on Miramichi River, New Brunswick. Died about 1800 in Tabusintac, New Brunswick. (Vancouver, 2004)

Holden, James – arrived in Shelburne, Nova Scotia on ship 'Apollo' from New York with Loyalists in 1783 (Nova Scotia, 2017)

Holder, Jacob – born in 1757 in Pennsylvania. Joined the Bucks County Volunteers in 1777 at Philadelphia which were sometimes attached to the Queens Rangers. To New Brunswick in 1783 with Loyalists. Died June 29, 1828 in Long Reach, Kings County, New Brunswick. (New Brunswick, 1980)

Horton, Jonathan – from New York. Went to Shelburne, Nova Scotia with Loyalists in 1783 and received land grant. (Nova Scotia, 2017)

Horton, Solomon – born in Westchester County, New York in 1736. Settled at Wallace, Cumberland County, Nova Scotia. Died November 14, 1816. (Victoria, 2017)

Howe, John, Sr. – Loyalist printer. Went to Halifax, Nova Scotia in 1776 from Boston. Returned to Rhode Island, then to New York and back to Halifax. Father of Joseph Howe. journalist, politician, premier, and lieutenant governor of Nova Scotia (Nova Scotia, 2019)

Humbert, Stephen – born in New Jersey in 1767. Arrived in Saint John, New Brunswick in 1783. Set up shop as a baker next to Trinity Church on Germain Street. One of chief organizers of Methodism in Saint John in 1791. (New Brunswick, 2008)

Hugh, Nicholas – born in Philadelphia, Pennsylvania in 1741. Joined British Army in 1776 with his wagon and horses. After war went to Saint John River in New Brunswick and then in 1786 to Prince Edward Island where settled at Murray Harbour. Died on November 17, 1831. (Abegweit, 1992)

I

Inglis, Bishop Charles – born 1734 in County Donegal, Ireland. To America as teacher. Became Anglican minister in New York. Preached loyalty to British Crown. Appointed first Bishop of British America. Died February 24, 1816 in Halifax and buried under St. Paul's Church. (Sir John Johnson, 1986)

Plate marking location of burial of Bishop Charles Inglis

in St. Paul's Church, Halifax, Nova Scotia

Ingraham, Hezekiah - born June 15, 1755 **in** Saybrook, Middlesex, Connecticut. Died June 14, 1826 in Margaree Valley, Cape Breton. Occupation: cooper. Appointed Justice of the Peace. **(Nova Scotia, 2020)**

J

Johnson, William –   Born in Guilford, New Haven, Connecticut. Died November 25, 1850 and buried at Waterford, Digby County, Nova Scotia aged 85. (Nova Scotia, 2017)

Waterford Cemetery in Digby County, Nova Scotia

Jones, Simeon – born in Weston, Massachusetts. Clerk of the Common Pleas in New Hampshire. Commissioned Lieutenant in King's American Dragoons. After American Revolution to Weymouth, Nova Scotia where farmed. Died August 17, 1823 and buried in St. Peter's Anglican Church cemetery. (Halifax- Dartmouth, 1984)

Judson, William – Family from Connecticut. Served in British Army during American Revolution. Died in Charlottetown on December 23, 1845. (Abegweit, 1973)

Headstone of Simeon Jones in St. Peter's Cemetery at

Weymouth North, Nova Scotia

L

Ladner, Andrew – born in Wurtemburg, Germany in late 1750s. Arrived in New York, met Edmund Fanning. Accompanied Fanning after war to Nova Scotia and then to Charlottetown in 1786 when he became Governor. (Toronto, 1999)

Legett, Captain John – born 1742 in North Carolina. Died December 11, 1812 at Country Harbour, Guysborough County, Nova Scotia. Captain in the Royal North Carolina Regiment and founder of the settlement of members of that corps, the South Carolina Royalists, and the King's Carolina Rangers at Country Harbour, Nova Scotia. (Halifax – Dartmouth, 2005)

Lloyd, Andrew – from Kinsale, Ireland. Born about 1752.   Served with Royal Fencible American Regiment. Died 1813 and buried in Chocolate Cove Cemetery, Charlotte County, New Brunswick. (Vancouver, 2010)

Lyman, Oliver – served in Loyalist company in West Florida. Born January 22, 1755. Came to Nova Scotia and granted town lot in Shelburne. After marriage moved to Wolfville, King's County, Nova Scotia. (Halifax- Dartmouth, 1983)

M

Magee, Henry –   born in Co. Armagh, Northern Ireland. Came to Pennsylvania before American Revolution. Buried in Oak Grove Cemetery, Kenville, Nova Scotia. Died 2, 1806. (Shelburne, 197

Mason, William - settled in Antigonish, Nova Scotia (Nova Scotia, 2018)

Maxwell, James –   born 1762 in County Armagh, Ireland and died August 26, 1847. He came to America in 1768 and settled near Philadelphia, Pennsylvania. In 1783 moved to Shelburne, Nova Scotia as Loyalist. He came to New Brunswick in 1784 and settled at Old Ridge, Saint Stephen Parish in Charlotte County. (Nova Scotia, 2018)

Melick, John – born 1752 in Somerset County, New Jersey. Died May 6, 1856 and buried in Fernhill Cemetery at Saint John, New Brunswick. (New Brunswick, 1985)

Melvin, Robert – born in Concord, Middlesex, Massachusetts. Died in Chester, Lunenburg County, Nova Scotia on July 24, 1787 (Nova Scotia, 2017)

Merritt, Robert – born in 1731 in Rye, New York. Member of Peter Hugeford's civilian militia Settled in Queens County, New Brunswick. Died in 1802 and buried in Merritt Cemetery at Hampstead, Queens County, New Brunswick. (Victoria, 2008)

Mills, Jesse – born about 1750 in Bedford, Westchester County, New York. Died in Cumberland County, Nova Scotia and buried in Linden Hillside Cemetery. (Nova Scotia, 2015)

Moore, James - born in Scotland in 1738. Arrived in Saint John, New Brunswick in 1783 from New York with Loyalists. Granted land as Loyalist in Kingston, New Brunswick. Died November 1820. (London & Western Ontario, 1984)

Murray, John, Sr. - born about 1735 in Scotland. To America where rented land in Harpersfield, Tryon County, New York. Indicted as Loyalist in 1777 and fled to New York. To Shelburne, Nova Scotia in 1783 and then in 1784 to Prince Edward Island. Settled on Bedeque Bay. (Vancouver, 2010)

N

Ness, Lieutenant John -   Served in Prince of Wales American Regiment. Settled in Maugerville, Sunbury County, New Brunswick (Victoria, 2013

Northrup, Benajah – born in 1752 in Fairfield County, Connecticut. Settled in Laugerville, Sunbury County, New Brunswick. Moved to Kingston in Kings County, New Brunswick. Died May 17, 1838 and buried in Trinity Anglican Cemetery there.   (New Brunswick, 2020)

O

Odell, Daniel – from Dutchess County, New York. Died in Springfield, Kings County, New Brunswick (New Brunswick, 2013)

Orser, William - born in 1763 in Westchester County, New York. Died December 24, 1844 and buried in Orser cemetery in Hartland, Carleton County, New Brunswick. (Halifax – Dartmouth,1996)

Outhouse, Robert – born 1750 from Westchester County, New York. Co – founder of Tiverton, Digby County, Nova Scotia (Nova Scotia, 2020)

Monument for Robert Outhouse in Hilltop Cemetery, Tiverton, Nova Scotia

P

Pearson, Thomas - born in 1754 in Frederick County, Virginia. Member of the Little River Regiment, Ninety – six Brigade. Left Charleston, South Carolina when evacuated in 1782. Settled in Hants County, Nova Scotia (Victoria, 2020)

Peers, Alexander -   born about 1745 in England. Died February 28, 1816 and buried in Dotten Cemetery at Wallace Bay, Cumberland County, Nova Scotia (Victoria, 2017)

Perry, Samuel -   Born in Sandstable, Barnwich, Massachusetts in 1735.
 Fled Massachusetts to Newport, Rhode Island in 1777 and joined the
Royal Associated Refugees. Died in Shelburne, Nova Scotia in 1829.
(Nova Scotia, 2014)

Peters, John Colonel. - born in 1740, in Hebron, Connecticut. He was
a Judge of Probate for the Court of Common Pleas and a Colonel of
the Gloucester County Militia in New York (today located in
northeastern Vermont). Appointed a member of Continental Congress
in 1774, but refused to take the office's oath of secrecy. In 1776 he fled
to Canada, where he was appointed colonel of the Queen's Loyal
Rangers by Sir Guy Carleton. Subsequently, his troops participated in
Burgoyne's campaign and engaged in combat with the Continental
Army during the Battle of Bennington. After the war his property was
confiscated as a consequence of his loyalist actions, so he and his family
remained in Canada, having settled at Cape Breton, Nova Scotia. About
1785, he went to England to enter his claim for reimbursement for
losses resulting from the confiscation of his property in the United
States. He was still in England when he died in 1788. (Nova Scotia,
2021)

Peters, Corporal Maurice -   from Long Island New York. Served with
Loyal American Regiment. Settled at Digby, Nova Scotia (Nova Scotia,
2017)

Pickering, William – born in Salem, Massachusetts in 1750. Settled at
New London, Prince Edward Island. Died June 30, 1837. (Abegweit,
1995)

Praught, Frederick – born 1729 and resided in Monmouth County,
New Jersey. Served as Private in James Rogers' King's Rangers First
Battalion. Granted 100 acres on lot 50, Prince Edward Island.
(Vancouver, 2012)

Prime, Michael – pioneer Loyalist settled at Grand Passage, Long Island, Digby County, Nova Scotia (Nova Scotia, 2020)

Prince, John - born in 1742 in Monmouth County, New Jersey. Came to New Brunswick in 1783 as Loyalist. Died August 17, 1825 and buried in Trinity Anglican Cemetery at Kingston, Kings County, New Brunswick.   (New Brunswick, 1987)

Purdy, Gabriel – born May 18, 1753 in White Plains, New York. Joined British Army and fought in Battle of White Plains, New York. Died May 8, 1841. After war settled at Westchester, Cumberland County, Nova Scotia named after his home in Westchester, New York. Buried in Rose Cemetery at Westchester. (Nova Scotia, 2020)

Q

Quereau, Joshua – New York Loyalist who settled at Granville, Annapolis County, Nova Scotia (Nova Scotia, 2020)

R

Raymond, Silas – born in 1748 in Fairfield County, Connecticut. Died on June 5,1824 and buried at Trinity Anglican Cemetery in Kingston, Kings County, New Brunswick.   (Toronto, 2007)

Robins, Richard – born about 1725, farmed in Monmouth County, New Jersey. Joined British forces at Trenton, captured and imprisoned. Upon release went to New York and departed with other Loyalists in 1783. Died February, 1785 at Sea Cow Head, Prince Edward Island. (Vancouver, 2009)

Robinson, Joseph – born in England in 1748. Settled in New York before war. Afterwards sailed to Shelburne, Nova Scotia and then to Prince Edward Island. Died at Charlottetown, Prince Edward Island on February 20, 1836. (Fredericton, 1973)

Rogers, Anthony - from Connecticut. Sailed after war from New York to Saint John, New Brunswick. (Kingston & District, 1985)

Ross, Private Donald – born about 1758, probably Scotland. Served with the Associated Departments of the Army and Navy Royal, North Carolina Regiment and Volunteers, Captain William Hamilton's Company. Died in 1842 in Guysborough, Nova Scotia. (Halifax - Dartmouth 2008)

Ruggles, Brigadier General Timothy –   born on October 20, 1711 in Rochester, Massachusetts. Graduated from Harvard in 1732. He was a military officer during the French and Indian War rising to the rank of brigadier general in 1758. Commanded the Loyal American Association in Boston. His estates were confiscated and he was named in the Massachusetts Banishment Act. In 1779 he received a grant of 10,000 acres of land in Wilmot, Nova Scotia where he settled. (Halifax - Dartmouth 2001)

Sign for Ruggles Road, Wilmot, Annapolis County, Nova Scotia named after

Brig. – Gen. Timothy Ruggles and family

Rulofson, Rulof -   born in Middlesex County, New Jersey in 1754. Served with 2nd Battalion, New Jersey Volunteers. Settled in Hampton, New Brunswick. Died Oct. 1, 1840. (Vancouver, 2011)

Rushton, John – from Westchester County, New York.   Settled on land granted in Westchester, Cumberland County, Nova Scotia. Died December 12, 1799. (Nova Scotia, 2016)

Schurman, William – born about 1743 in New Rochelle, New York. At end of war sailed to Shelburne, Nova Scotia and then on to Prince Edward Island. Settled at Bedeque. Died on September 15, 1819. (Abegweit, 1984)

Seaman, Jacomiah - born 1735 **in** Westchester County, New York. Died on August 23 1808 **in** Fanningsburough (now Wallace) Cumberland, Nova Scotia (Nova Scotia, 2018)

Seeley, Seth - born in 1737 in Stanford, Connecticut and came to New Brunswick in 1783. Settled on Long Reach, Kings County. Died May 6, 1823. (New Brunswick, 1982)

Sharp, Samuel - born 1741 in Woodbridge, New Jersey. Recruiting Sergeant for Loyal American Regiment at Staten Island, New York. Arrived in Saint John, New Brunswick in 1783. (Fredericton, 1999)

Siteman, Henry - Heinrich Seidemann, known in North America as Henry Siteman, born May 11, 1741 in Germany. He immigrated to South Carolina. Served in Loyalist regiments. Evacuated Charleston with British forces and arrived at Halifax about November 1782. He was one of the organizers in Halifax of the Associated Loyalists of South Carolina. Moved to Ship Harbour in May 1783. Died there in 1813. (Nova Scotia, 2017)

Sparling, Peter William – born in 1732 and died 1821. From New York settled in North Sydney, Cape Breton. (Nova Scotia, 2021)

Strang, Jesse - born about 1763 at White Plains, Westchester County, New York. Sailed to Shelburne in fall of 1783 and to Prince Edward Island in July, 1784 with other Loyalists including William Schurman and settled at Bedeque. (Vancouver, 2018)

Stymiest, Benjamin Sr. - born April 17, 1731 at Gravesend, Kings County, New York. Evacuated from New York. Arrived in New Brunswick. Died September 18, 1823 and buried in St. John the Evangelist Anglican Cemetery Old in Bay du Vin, Northumberland County, New Brunswick (Vancouver, 2008)

T

Teed, Moses -   born in Westchester County, New York about 1762. Died about 1840 in Wallace, Cumberland County, Nova Scotia (Victoria, 2017)

Tuttle, Stephen Sr. – from New Jersey, born 1733. but moved to New York. Settled in Wallace, Cumberland County, Nova Scotia. Died 1818. (Nova Scotia 2015)

U

Underhill, Nathaniel – born in 1751 in Westchester County, New York. Died in December, 2006 in Fredericton, New Brunswick and buried there in Old Burial Ground. (Fredericton, 1975)

Underhill, William - from Westchester County, New York. Served in Queens Ranges. Settled at Wickham Parish, Queens County, New Brunswick (Victoria, 2009)

V

Van Buskirk, Andrew –   from New Jersey to Nova Scotia (Nova Scotia 2018)

Van Buskirk, Lawrence - born in Hackensack, New Jersey on April 20, 1728. Settled at Aylesford, King's County, Nova Scotia. Went to Saint John, New Brunswick as Loyalist in 1783 and then to Nova Scotia (Nova Scotia, 2020)

Van Iderstine, John – born in Bergen County, New Jersey. Served in 4th Battalion, New Jersey Volunteers. Sailed to Shelburne, Nova Scotia in 1783 where stayed for one year. Went to Prince Edward Island and received grant of land near head of Vernon River. (Abegweit, 2018)

W

Webb, Noah – born November 29, 1754 in Stanford, Connecticut. He joined Captain Purdy's Corps of Westchester Refugees and Militia. Died in Wallace, Cumberland County, Nova Scotia on January 18, 1832. (Nova Scotia, 2017)

Winslow, Edward – born at Plymouth, Massachusetts on February 20, 1746. Graduated from Harvard. Appointed Collector of Customs for Boston and Registrar of Probate. Evacuated to Halifax in 1776. He took Coat of Arms of Council Chamber which now hang on wall in Trinity Church at Saint John, New Brunswick. Appointed Muster

General to loyalist troops and then Lieutenant colonel of Loyalist
Association Refugees in Rhode Island. In 1783 sailed to Annapolis,
Nova Scotia then appointment in Halifax, followed by Saint John. In
1807 appointed to the Supreme Court Bench of New Brunswick. He
died on June 9, 1784 and was buried in Halifax. (Halifax - Dartmouth,
1983)

"Sacred to the memory of Edward Winslow, Esquire, who died
the 9th of June, 1784, in the 72nd year of his age. Descended
from a race of ancestors, Governors of the ancient Colony of Plymouth,
he in no one instance degenerated from their loyalty or
virtue, but while he filled the first offices, became as conspicuous
by public integrity as he was amiable in the milder shades of
private life. Although his fortunes suffered shipwreck in the storm of
Civil War, and he forsook his native country from an
attachment to his sovereign, neither his cheerful manners nor the
calm reward of conscious rectitude forsook him in old age. He
died as he lived, beloved by his friends and respected by his enemies."
(14)

(14) Transcription in The Winslow Papers, 1776-1826

Gravestone in Old Burying Ground at Halifax, NS of Edward Winslow

Wood, Samuel – born about 1725 on Long Island, New York. Served in the Queen's Rangers. Buried in the Old Harrison Burying Ground in Macaan, Nova Scotia. (Victoria, 2005)

Wright, William – from Westchester County, New York. Settled in North Bedeque, Prince Edward Island. Identified as Loyalist and imprisoned for 12 months. Left New York for Shelburne, Nova Scotia in 1783 and then moved on to Prince Edward Island with William Schurman to settle in Bedeque area. Died in February, 1819. (Col. Edward Jessup, 2002)

Y

Yerxa, John – born in 1751 at Westchester County, New York. Died June 11, 1828 and buried in Keswick Cemetery, York County, New Brunswick (Victoria, 2010)

5. APPENDIX A -Who were the Loyalists of the American Revolution? By W.C. Mikel

The author of this article, William Charles Mikel, was President of the Belleville Loyalists and served as Vice - President of the United Empire Loyalists' Association. He was a descendant of Godlove Mikel, a U.E. Loyalist who settled at Ameliasburgh, Ontario. He was also a lawyer, elected President of the Ontario Bar Association in 1912, and later Mayor for Belleville, Ontario in 1924, then appointed Magistrate in 1926. To mark the 150th arrival of the Loyalists in 1924 led a group to construct a monument to the Loyalists in downtown Belleville.

Old Postcard with monument to United Empire Loyalists in Belleville, Ontario

Who were the Loyalists of the American Revolution?
Not until 1914 that Words "United Empire Loyalist" received official
sanction
By W.C. Mikel
Published in The Kingston Whig Standard Newspaper. 27 February
1935, page 20

Who were the Loyalists of the American Revolution? How are they
ascertained? These are two questions that are occasionally asked.
During February the radio and press have dealt with Washington and
Lincoln very fully. It may not be remiss now to refer to things
Canadian.

Prior to the Declaration of Independence on the 4th of July 1776
undoubtedly the majority of residents of the thirteen colonies were
loyal to Great Britain in sentiment. At the Continental Congress of
July,1776 the vote of separation was a tie. At the adjourned meeting
July 4, 1776 the vote was one majority in favor of separation, following
which the vote was made unanimous.

This close vote no doubt reflected the sentiment of the people. In 1775
the Continental Congress declared that there was no truth in the
assertion that the people of the colonies as a whole desired separation.
After the war started the sentiment changed considerably in favor of
separation, and after the battle of Yorktown in 1781, which was really
won by the French, the sentiment became much stronger in favor of
separation. Dr. Caniff says that some 20,000 Loyalists poured into the
colony of Quebec, which then included what is now Ontario. Van
Tyne, a U.S. historian, places the number at 25,000 and also estimates
the total migration to all British territories at about 60,000.

After the constitution of the United States was adopted in 1787 those
who remained in the new republic became citizens of it, and could no
longer be regarded as Loyalists, whatever their earlier sentiments may
have been. The Loyalists who came to this country may be divided into
six general heads:

1. The Unity of Empire Loyalists or Mark of Honor Loyalists
constituted under the Order - in - Council passed by Lord Dorchester
at Quebec on the 9th of November, 1789. These comprised persons
who had joined the Royal Standard prior to the close of the Revolution
and after the Revolution came to this country, including their
descendants. Membership in this class does not depend on registration
under the Land Boards as that registration was primarily for the
purpose of acquiring land. In those days as there were no roads travel
through the bush was exceedingly difficult or impossible, and travel by
water was also difficult because of the absence of the supply of lumber
and nails with which to construct boats and writing material was almost
unprocurable consequently many of these Loyalists never registered;
only about 7,000 registered with the Land Boards. Some 5,000 filed
claims with the Royal Commission many of whom had already
registered with the Land Boards.

2. An Order was passed by Colonel John Graves Simcoe, Lieutenant
Governor in Council, on the 6th of April, 1796, extending the time for
registration.

3. On the 31st day of October, 1806, Francis Gore, Lieutenant
Governor in Council, had an order passed extending the time for
registration for land to the quarter sessions at Michaelmass. In none of
these orders were the words "United Empire Loyalists" used.

4. The Royal Commission Loyalists. The British Government in July,
1783 appointed a Royal Commission to hear claims of the Loyalists of

the American Revolution for compensation. The commission classified the Loyalists under six different classes as follows:

(a) Those who had rendered services to Great Britain;

(b) Those who had borne arms against the Revolution;

(c) Uniform Loyalists;

(d) Loyalists resident in Great Britain;

(e) Those who took the oath of allegiance to American states but afterwards joined the British;

(f) Those who took arms with the Americans and later joined the British army and navy.

None of these were called "United Empire Loyalists".

5. On the 27th of May, 1914, the Dominion Parliament passed a statute incorporating the United Empire Loyalists' Association of Canada. This was the first occasion when the words "United Empire Loyalists" were used legally and this statute extended the term to include the "descendants of those families who during the American Revolutionary War of 1775 to 1783 sacrificed their homes in retaining their loyalty to the British Crown."

6. The name United Empire Loyalist has been used by writers and speakers prior to this date, but up to this time the term had never received recognition as a matter of law.

6. FURTHER REFERENCE:

Articles:

"Our Loyalist Ancestors – Biographical Sketches of Loyalist Ancestors by the Membership", A bicentennial project of the Halifax – Dartmouth branch of the United Empire Loyalists' Association of Canada, 1983

McConnell, Brian, "The Hon. Alfred Gilpin Jones & the Loyalists of Nova Scotia". https://www.uelac.org/Loyalist-Info/extras/Jones-Elisha/Hon-Alfred-Gilpin-Jones-and-the-Loyali sts-of-Nova-Scotia-by-Brian-McConnell.pdf

McConnell, Brian, "Loyal Then - Loyal Now", http://www.uelac.org/events/Loyal-Then-Loyal-Now-by-Brian-McConnell.pdf

Books:

Haslam, Doris and Jones, Orlo, "An Island Refuge – Loyalists and Disbanded Troops on the Island of Saint John", published by Abegweit Branch of the United Empire Loyalists' Association of Canada, 1983

Hayward, Frederick H., "100 Years of the UELAC", Global Heritage Press, 2014

Mathews, Hazel C, "The Mark of Honour", University of Toronto Press, 1965

Merriman, Brenda Dougall, "United Empire Loyalists, A Guide to Tracing Loyalist Ancestors in Upper Canada", Global Heritage Press, 2006

Pipes, Gail Bonsall, "Loyalists All", published by the New

Brunswick Branch of the United Empire Loyalists'
Association of Canada, 1985

Reid, William D., "The Loyalists in Ontario – The Sons and
Daughters of The American Loyalists of Upper Canada",
Hunterdon House, 1973

"The Loyalists of the Eastern Townships in Quebec"
published for Sir John Johnson Centennial Branch by
Progressive Publications (1970) Incorporated, 1984

"The Loyalists of Quebec, 1774 – 1825 – A Forgotten
History", published under auspices of Heritage Branch –
Montreal of the United Empire Loyalist Association of
Canada by Price Patterson Ltd., 1989

"The Old United Empire Loyalists List", originally
published by the Centennial Committee of the United
Empire Loyalists, reprinted by Clearfield Co., 1984

Walker, James W. St.G., "The Black Loyalists", University
of Toronto Press, 1992

Videos:

 "Certificate of Loyalist Descent (United Empire Loyalists)"
by Brian McConnell, UE
https://www.youtube.com/watch?v=6AykLFrk3v8

"United Empire Loyalist Certificate of Descent Presentation"
by Brian McConnell, UE
https://www.youtube.com/watch?v=yZzhpi1I_w0

Websites:

Loyalist Migrations https://loyalistmigrations-westernu.opendata.arcgis.com/

Loyalists – Library and Archives Canada https://www.bac-lac.gc.ca/eng/discover/military-heritage/loyalists/Pages/introduction.aspx

The Loyalist Collection, University of New Brunswick https://loyalist.lib.unb.ca/home

The On-Line Institute for Advanced Loyalist Studies http://www.royalprovincial.com/

United Empire Loyalists' Association of Canada https://uelac.ca/

7. INDEX

Bower, Adam, 50

Bower, Charles, 51

Bowlby, Richard, 51

Braddock, Samuel, 51

Brittain, Joseph, 51

Brooks, Abraham, 51

Brunson, Daniel, 52

Buckman, Samuel, 52

Burlock, Job, 52

Campbell, Colin, 52

Chandler, Joshua, 53

Chase, James, 54

Church, Charles, 54

Colter, William, 54

Cowperthwaite, Hugh, 54

Craig, Private John, 54

Craig, James, 55

Crawford, Edward, 55

8. ABOUT THE AUTHOR

Brian McConnell, UE, B.A. (Hons) LL.B. is an Historian and Author of nine nonfiction history books. He is the sixth great grandson of a soldier who served withs Jessup's Corps and the Loyal Rangers during the American Revolution, afterwards settling near Prescott, Ontario as a United Empire Loyalist. As a member of the United Empire Loyalists' Association of Canada he has served as Secretary and then President of the Nova Scotia Branch as well as a Dominion Trustee and Atlantic Regional Vice – President. He has also been a re – enactor in the 84th Regiment of Foot (Royal Highland Emigrants) and the King's Orange Rangers, two loyalist groups from the American Revolution.

Brian McConnell behind headstone for Henry Magee

in Oak Grove Cemetery, Kentville, Nova Scotia

OTHER BOOKS PUBLISHED BY THIS AUTHOR:

1)   Loyalist History of Nova Scotia; On the Loyalist Trail

2. **Loyalist Cemeteries & Gravestones of Nova Scotia:
    Annapolis & Digby Counties;**

3.   The Loyalists of Digby;

4.   Old St. Edward's Church & the Loyalists

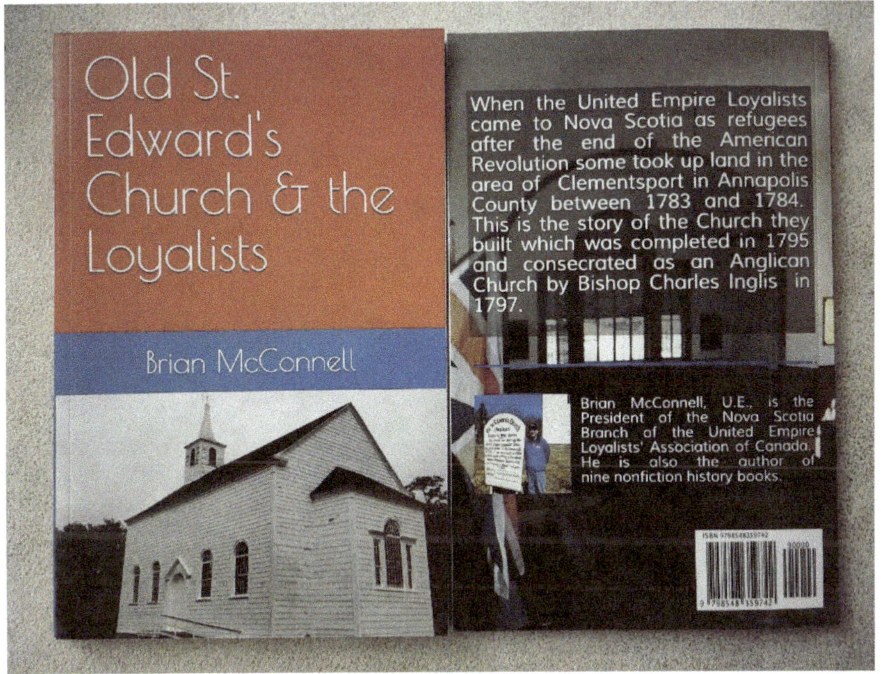

www.ingramcontent.com/pod-product-compliance
Lightning Source LLC
Chambersburg PA
CBHW050035260726

48658CB00005B/1612